YOUR TIME HAS COME

Also by Joshua Beckman

Things Are Happening
Something I Expected To Be Different
Nice Hat. Thanks. (with Matthew Rohrer)

YOUR TIME HAS COME

Joshua Beckman

Verse Press
Amherst, MA
2004

Published by Verse Press
Copyright © 2004 by Joshua Beckman
All rights reserved.

Library of Congress Cataloging-in-Publication Data

Beckman, Joshua.
  Your time has come / Joshua Beckman. — 1st ed.
    p. cm.
  ISBN 0-9723487-5-1 (pbk. : alk. paper)
  I. Title.
  PS3552.E2839Y68 2003
  811'.54—dc21   2003012944

Printed in Canada
Cover design by Sam Potts
Interior type composed by Bent Graphics

9 8 7 6 5 4 3 2
First edition

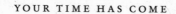
YOUR TIME HAS COME

Come up from the subway
and there it's just glass.

Light from the ferry's window
mixed along the floor.
Alone we wait to be delivered.

Two new sparrows—
the tourists don't know
they're new.

That Russian boat
goes everywhere
and then sits here
still and peaceful.

They'll spend the summer
crushing the garden—
a steam let off slowly.

Seagulls beside ferry boat.
They're people-watching.

She thought there were too many poems—
now she's lonely
waiting to write one.

Mr. Crazy stands
in the elevator
wanting my opinion.

Up on the fire escape
I was thinking how to live
another day without a job.

He died so young,
I should tell him
what happened.

Oh atlas
look
you forgot my island.

They keep calling
but I'll just sweat it out here
in my little apartment.

Antic motorboat
we're not impressed
with your speeding.

Lightning hit the island
so I left with the birds
to watch it from here.

A quiet rain
soaked my books—
even the dogs
didn't see it coming.

Late at night
the TV flashing.

No money left,
then just tell a good story.

On couch,
searching for nickels,
storm echoes.

Too tired to write
and this hot apartment
keeps me awake.

Mice in walls.
Better there
than here.

I won't miss that gnawing
but I probably won't forget either.

Rain over Jersey
we watched you
from the roof.

Cigarettes will kill you.
She said it so sweetly
I wanted another.

They could take over the place,
but the mice can't tell
when I've gone away.

The sound of children
outside my window—
come and listen.

One song after another,
those singers
seemed so lonely.

Why want quiet
and then
keep asking that question.

Mouse on two feet,
your time has come!

On boat
with umbrella
feeling practical.

Indians swimming
in Manhattan Bay
years ago.

These poems won't work
with memory,
so why won't you call?

A Filipino freighter
filled the city
with Filipino stuff.

Ferry moving quickly,
blessed fish's memory.

Over Kill Van Kull
Jersey stacks smoke
all night long.

Yeah I live here,
but so does that rotten television.

Sweat all day—
the sun doesn't
like you either.

Rotten pad,
you're too small
for so many poems.

Manhattan, gathered by water,
you are useless buildings
and only slightly salty.

Sure
you're waking up somewhere strange
but I do that every day.

The air is always there
and my fan
knows just what to do with it.

Those people were like ants,
waiting for me to say something stupid
they could drag back home with them.

I'm no better than anyone else,
but I could be less afraid.

Don't be concerned,
live another week
and then be concerned.

Chris can't even remember
what he said to me,
and now he wants something new.

Hum of the universe
I'm trying to sleep.

Sad story,
my shoes sitting at the end of the room
and me looking at them.

You didn't know me
so why did I think
acting like someone else
would be more interesting.

I wanted contemplation
and foolishly
grabbed for my pen.

Now that I'm older
the hot sun reminds me of other hot suns.
Years ago it burned.

The missionary on the boat
was so beautifully patient,
but it wasn't his God
that made him that way.

After dinner
the missionaries don't talk about God,
they talk about us.

I will sleep
and you will tell me about it
later.

Spring in sandals.
Summer in sandals.
Who do you love?

Mr. Crazy
knows it's summer—
why else sit on the corner.

Jonesing all day
and kids on the boat
playing with a dime bag.

It's a chill
and a rain beyond the island,
mostly a chill.

That memory is so crushing,
why write me letters
I already know.

Foolish boat
ignoring the water
you push through.

Getting mean over quarters,
then tearing the chicken apart,
is it really me?

Light darts about the cabin.
Out from the coast
waves play, unprepared.

I keep thinking
of that one time over and over again.
Is that shallow or deep?

Plants in hallway
near empty elevator,
I'll save you.

He imagined a satellite
passing by nightly.
I'll look too.

Talking about the weather
became trite,
which was sad.

Someone planted all those flowers
and I like them.

That's perfume.
I'd know it anywhere
by its smell.

It stopped raining.
Now let's bring the moped
crosstown.

Mike's late to the bar.
The park is warm and empty.
He better not be there.

Foreign kissing couple
you could have done that
anywhere.

The bird was more interested in them
than I was.
And I knew what they were doing.

Even the mean waitress
feels the breeze.

I think you will hate
the neighborhood,
but visit anyway.

I was early
and watched the people rushing.
Be early more often.

Some man on a bicycle
playing his radio.
What world doesn't he rule.

No one sleeps
above the water.
Let's try this summer.

Behind the building
summer's bitter grasses
and afternoon approaching.

Tiny plants
slightly folded—
a stream let off
the sound of birds.

Twisting river,
from up here
your deception seems honest.

Every time I leave the house
I write a poem—
but I was there all day.

She was so sweet
and happy to see me—
all because of some little story
you told her.

All day on the ocean
without finding anything.
That will help them sleep.

Sun off the heads of a thousand cars
and one white van in a ditch
with sun shining off it too.

Mad happy swallow
where'd you find that friend?

A new boat sleeps in that place
each night.
The current there must be mild.

To watch you open
and to know you'll open and close again.
All is flora.

It felt so good
to get my sunburn,
but now I've got it.

Flying a kite
off his roof—
I'm worried he'll fall.

So hot tonight
even the cops eat ice cream.

A bad accident
preparing to meet me,
it knows how I think.

The fan keeps me cool
and outside light
burns all the dead weeds.

Sun, today
the smart made shorts
from pants.

In my new apartment
this morning
someone different.

Fog horn
and empty freighter.
Along the coast
a mild sun.

Train rushing to Chelsea
is thinking like me.

Waking late
in the high gray morning,
traffic passing.

What's so funny
about peace love and
understanding?
Good question.

Some barge called The Maya
pushed through the bay.
Our promenade was the sweetest promenade.

Don't be mad,
I'm in bed thinking
of you at work.

Are you enjoying
getting in trouble
for what we did last night?

It's just a season—
they always come back.

Leaves rotting
out beyond the city—
a dog resting in that heat.

Storm waiting
for her to leave,
then raining.

They think school
will make them smarter.
I like how they think that.

Some guy trying
to get the game on the radio—
now we all want to hear it.

Did everyone skip work
today
or is it just me?

We could power a city
with this energy,
but it'd be a waste.

They let me out
of the bar to think
but I went right back in.

Long night
and I'm crying for home,
wherever that is.

Those drugs don't have anything
to do with our happiness.
Now I really sound like a junky.

In the hills
light filling the hills
a moment before I meet anyone.

We went on what we had to go on.
The sun and thoughts
similar to older thoughts.

Clouds casting small shadows
on fields.

Behind my parents' house
wind moves ferns
in chorus with singing birds.

Hidden in low shrubs
the stream still flows,
though now it's the birds we hear.

They say the sun will burn the fog off.
Long days of that happening
to come.

River by highway,
year after year I forget you,
but someone doesn't.

Before she returned
I stepped slowly through the yard
as if to say, here an entire hour passes.

Morning
and deer quietly crush herbs
as they walk to the river.

Branches down
in harmless bunches.
Phone lines and rain.

The smell of them painting boats
and of damp shade, moss.
From this car
we watch everything.

Acting crazy
after rain
the birds
just like home.

What if the fog is gone
when I get back?
I'll probably forget, that's what.

If a tree falls
in the woods etc.
and so too with friends.

Hour after hour
of hot sun,
all I have left—ideas.

When you return
and perfect your stories
it seems so sad.

Quiet birds—
we still have hours of sleep
and of wakefulness.

One layer after another,
lush trees set the stage
for some green play of birds.

Today they waved at us for fun.
I wouldn't have any of it.
That's me, all self-important and lonely.

I need to get out
from under all this thinking,
where've you been hiding?

Returning to Staten Island
and that weak moan—
a foghorn miles away.

They let the TV go all night
and just sat on the stoop ignoring it.

Are you gone
or is it just me
paying attention to roving drunks
and laughing with them?

Two bikes in a pile.
I've been away
and they've been waiting.

Clouds gather
over Wall Street
for lunch.

Some hippie
thought I was an accountant.
Maybe he's right.

How strange to be fighting
this voice
when it speaks.

Friends meet in the city.
I'll wait here for two days
then start writing.

I love how people keep dying
and I can spend all day
thinking about her petty comment.

Everyone's got a lover
waiting to come back
mystically changed.

So my day is set,
I'll smoke something
and walk around.

Who knows what everyone's doing tonight.
Well, I'm in bed
trying to write these poems.

The phone just waited there
to pull me in
to your sad complaint.

Sore feet.
I was so stoned
I walked all the way home.

Twice a day distrust,
twice again tomorrow—
no wind can blow it away.

Hot concrete
after rain.

Today I'll spend the day
stopping myself
from doing what I want.

Arcade of light
laid down on water.
A sea of strangers
stand around.

I don't care
about anyone else this week,
but I'm not complaining.

Back to the city
the cool wind
and the cleanest air
seemed so temporary.

I wanted to stop writing
and the poem said
it's a beautiful blue night
stop writing.

JOSHUA BECKMAN was born in New Haven, Connecticut. He is the author of *Things Are Happening*, *Something I Expected To Be Different*, and two collaborations with Matthew Rohrer: *Nice Hat. Thanks.* and *Adventures While Preaching the Gospel of Beauty* (an audio CD released in 2003). He lives in Staten Island.

Poems from this book first appeared in *Both*, *The Canary*, *Castagraf*, *Crowd*, *Hayden's Ferry Review*, *Jubilat*, *La Petite Zine*, *Skanky Possum*, *Slope* and *Swerve*. The author wishes to thank the editors of these publications as well as his family and friends.